baechtold's best

AFGHANISTAN

the ultimate visual travel guide

Abrams Image

CONTENTS

A NIGHT ON THE RIVER BOOM

Northwest of Afghanistan flows a river. The River Boom. One afternoon in the spring of 2002, right after sunset, Swiss graphic designer Claude Baechtold found himself in the back of a four-wheel-drive, stranded on the narrow riverbank by the mounting waters of the river that had already eaten a few curves of the dirt road. Another car was stuck with them. Out of it nonchalantly came a warlord, armed to the teeth, to borrow Mr. Baechtold's sleeping bag and wish him a good night. The cautious driver advised Mr. Baechtold to neither go out nor to make a noise, because the area was infested by wolves and by stray Taliban fighters. In the meantime, the River Boom's furious waters had risen by three feet and big rocks were falling from the cliff just above the road, some of them precisely the size of the car. Mr. Baechtold, who was accompanying two unimpressed foreign reporters, did not get much sleep that night. But by the crack of dawn, he had come up with a great idea.

The many books he had read about this country included some vintage tourist guides from the time Afghanistan was well known on the backpacking circuit for its unparalleled hospitality, fantastic food, great hiking and . . . um . . . legendary hashish, but none of those gave him a clue about what he would actually find in the country. Why? Because these books were lacking pictures. When he woke up by the River Boom, pleasantly surprised to be alive, Mr. Baechtold had decided to create a series of guides made only of pictures. He then started to take photos of practically everything he saw, to give travelers a real taste of this country shrouded in myth and mystery, a country that actually is the ultimate independent traveler's frontier. Whether it's spellbinding Kabul, mystic Herat, the alluring snow-covered peaks of the Hindu Kush, or the sun-baked deserts, his carefully researched picture guide will provide all the down-to-earth advice you'll need to explore this versatile but spectacular destination.

Next page: Kabul airport

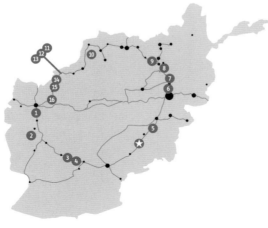

⭐ Road between Qalat and Moqor

ASPHALT

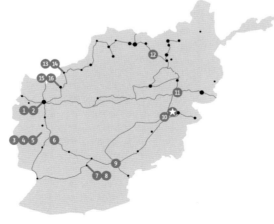

⭐ Zanagha, 20 kilometers (13 miles) northeast of Ghazni

BEARD

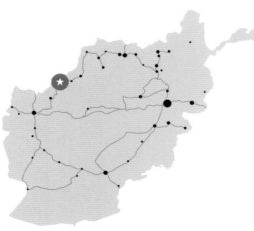

⭐ On the road between Ghowrmach and Bala Morghab

BLUE HILL

⭐ Kabul, Kart-e Char neighborhood

BROKEN THING

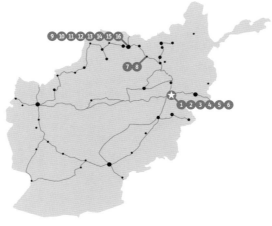

★ Kabul, Wazir Akbar Khan neighborhood

BURKA

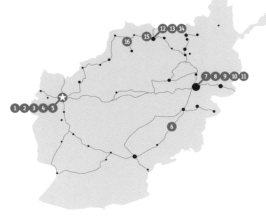

✪ Herat, outside the wall of Masjid-e Jameh mosque

CART

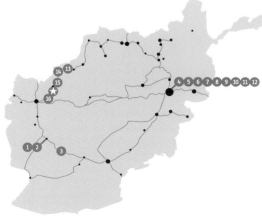

✪ On the road between Qala-e Now and the Sabzak Pass

CHILD

✪ Ghazni, Governor's bodyguard

CUSTOMIZED AK

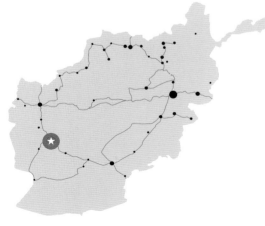

⭐ Wall decoration of Farah Rud restaurant, poster representing Singapore

DREAM

❶ Porto ❷ Mecca ❸ Switzerland ❹ Dubai
❺ Malaysia ❻ Composition by Mr. Raza ❼ Singapore ❽ Switzerland
❾ Switzerland ❿ Singapore ⓫ Germany ⓬ Malaysia
⓭ Jordan ⓮ Switzerland ⓯ Malaysia ⓰ Singapore

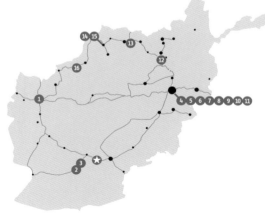

⭐ Checkpoint between Gereshk and Kandahar

GENERAL

① Herat ② Khoft 62 ③ Lashkar Gah ④ Kabul
⑤ Kabul ⑥ Kabul ⑦ Kabul ⑧ Kabul
⑨ Kabul ⑩ Kabul ⑪ Kabul ⑫ Pol-e Khomri
⑬ Mazar-e Sharif ⑭ Sheberghan ⑮ Sheberghan ⑯ Qeysar

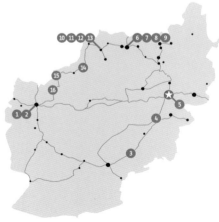

⭐ Kabul, Dreamland Guest House, Shar-e Now neighborhood

HOTEL ROOM

① Herat
   Hotel Mowafaq

② Herat
   Hotel Marco Polo

③ Qalat
   Gov. Hafizullah's guesthouse

④ Ghazni
   Sufi Sheikh's private home

⑤ Kabul, Shar-e Now
   Italia guesthouse

⑥ Mazar-e Sharif
   Barat Hotel, room 43

⑦ Mazar-e Sharif
   Uzbek leader's private home

⑧ Mazar-e Sharif
   Barat Hotel, room 56

⑨ Mazar-e Sharif
   Barat Hotel, room 45

⑩ Sheberghan
   Sheberghan Hotel, room 2

⑪ Sheberghan
   Sheberghan Hotel, room 3

⑫ Sheberghan
   General Dostum's guesthouse

⑬ Sheberghan
   unnamed truckers' inn

⑭ Meymaneh
   WFP guesthouse

⑮ Bala Morghab
   Oxfam office

⑯ Qala-e Now
   municipality's guesthouse

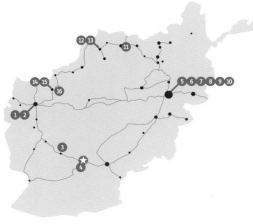

✪ Gereshk, restaurant at the southern exit of the city

INTERIOR

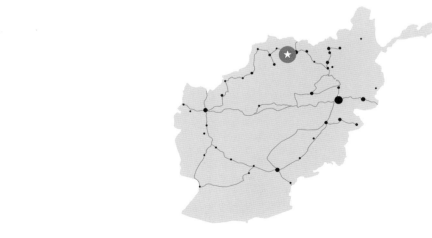

✪ Marijuana field, 30 kilometers (19 miles) west of Mazar-e Sharif

MARIJUANA

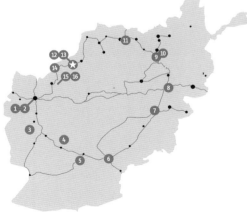

⭐ Qeysar, Fatulah Khan's dewan

MEAL

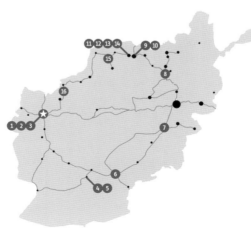

✪ Herat, one of the Musalla Minarets

MONUMENT

⭐ Main road to Kandahar, between Chah-e Chahan and Farah Rud

MOUNTAIN

① Herat (airport)　　② Herat – Adraskan　　③ Zirkuh Valley　　④ Delaram – Khadji Sattar
⑤ Delaram – Gereshk　　⑥ Gereshk – Kandahar　　⑦ Kandahar　　⑧ Kandahar
⑨ Moqor – Ghazni　　⑩ Ghazni – Kabul　　⑪ Salang Tunnel – Khenjan　　⑫ Salang Tunnel – Khenjan
⑬ Samangan – Kholm　　⑭ Sheberghan – Meymaneh　　⑮ Meymaneh – Qeysar　　⑯ Sabzak Pass

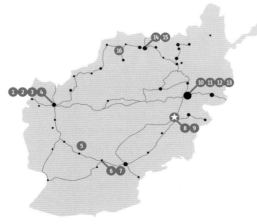

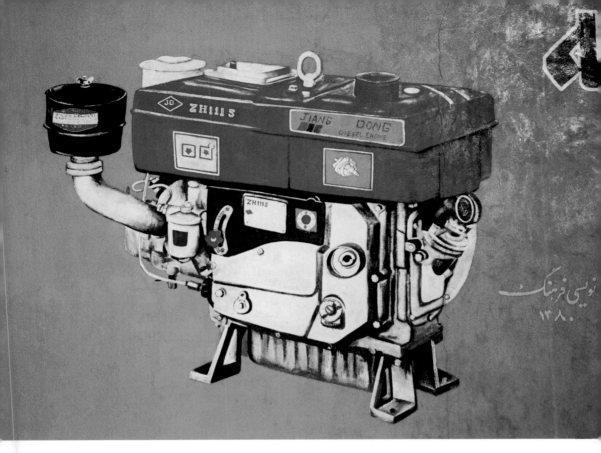

✪ Ghazni, northern exit of the city, toward Kabul

MURAL

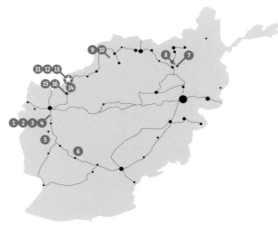

✪ Bala Morghab

PET

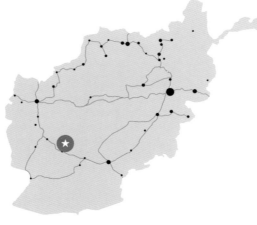

⭐ Khadji Sattar, poppy field about 15 kilometers (9 miles) north of Delaram

POPPY

✪ On the road between Samangan and Kholm

PYLON

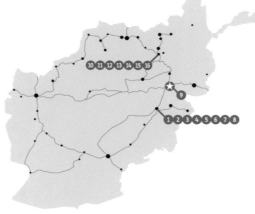

⭐ Kabul, Shar-e Now neighborhood

RADIATOR

⭐ On the road between Chechaktu and Ghowrmach

RED VALLEY

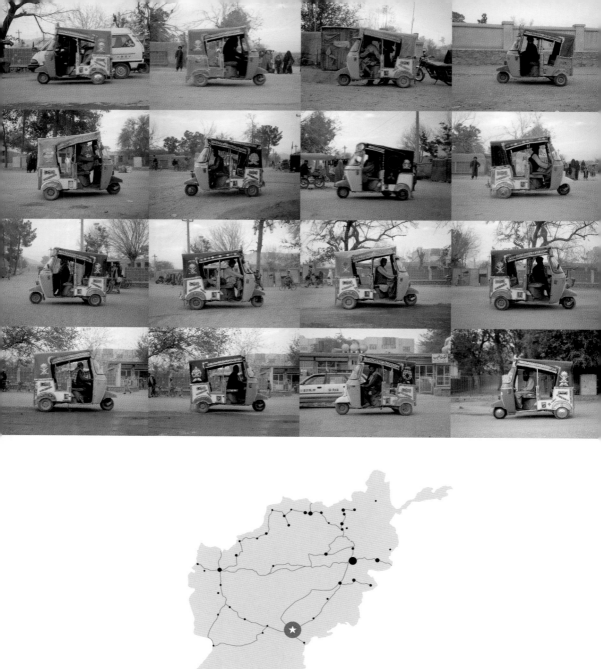

★ Kandahar, main road

RICKSHAW

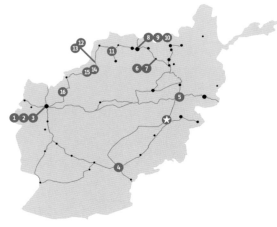

✪ Ghazni, on the way to the American base, first checkpoint

RUSSIAN JEEP

1. Herat
2. Herat
3. Herat
4. Kandahar
5. Kabul
6. Samangan
7. Samangan
8. Mazar-e Sharif
9. Mazar-e Sharif
10. Mazar-e Sharif
11. Sheberghan
12. Faizabad
13. Kuh-e Sayyad
14. Meymaneh
15. Almar
16. Qala-e Now

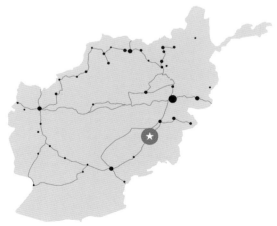

⭐ Moqor, road to Kabul

SANDSTORM

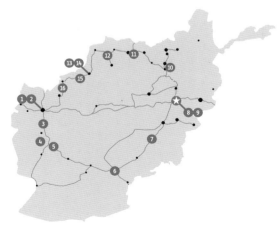

⭐ Kabul, Mikrorayon neighborhood

SKY

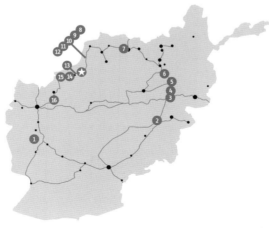

⭐ Road between Meymaneh and Almar

SOVIET TANK

⭐ Mazar-e Sharif, in front of Barat Hotel

TAXI

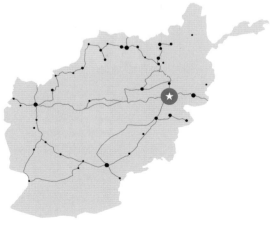

Kabul, Mikrorayon neighborhood

TEENAGER

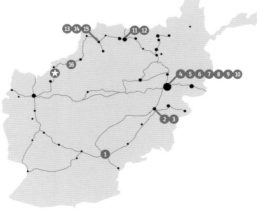

⭐ 5 kilometers (3 miles) north of Daria-e Boom, at the River Boom

UNIFORM

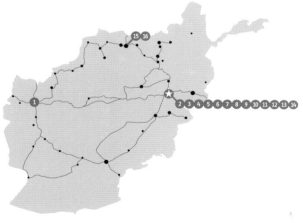

★ Kabul, Kart-e Char neighborhood

VILLA

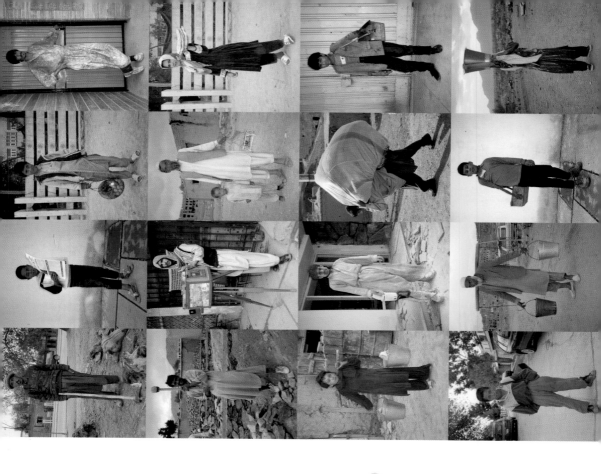

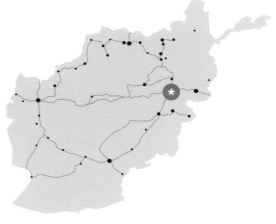

⭐ Kabul, Kart-e Char neighborhood

WORKER

Editor : Deborah Aaronson
Concept and Design : Claude Baechtold
Photography: Claude Baechtold
Maps: Aurélie Boissière
Headline typeface: Cargo (www.optimo.ch)
Production Manager : Kaija Markoe

Library of Congress Cataloging-in-Publication Data

Baechtold's best Afghanistan : the ultimate visual travel guide.
    p. cm.
 ISBN 0-8109-9223-X (pbk. with flaps)
 1. Afghanistan-Guidebooks. 2. Afghanistan-Pictorial works. 3. Afghanistan-Maps.

 DS351.B34 2006
 915.8104'470222-dc22

          2005025644

Published in 2006 by Abrams Image, an imprint of Harry N. Abrams, Inc.

Printed and bound in China
10 9 8 7 6 5 4 3 2 1

HNA ▪▮▮▮▮▮
harry n. abrams, inc.
a subsidiary of La Martinière Groupe
115 West 18th Street
New York, NY 10011
www.hnabooks.com

Warning

Afghanistan remains unsafe, especially outside Kabul. US-led military operations against Taliban forces are ongoing. Acts of violence, often targeting foreigners, continue. Landmines, banditry, and ethno-political conflict add to the grim picture. Visitors should maintain a high level of security awareness, avoid demonstrations, avoid traveling alone and in the dark, and contact their consular representative for the latest information.